on the drag strip

on the drag strip

by E. and R. S. Radlauer

illustrated with photographs by the authors

Franklin Watts, Inc., 845 Third Avenue, New York, New York 10022
SBN 531-01995-0. Copyright © 1971 by E. and R. S. Radlauer
Library of Congress Catalog Card Number: 70-151889. Printed in the United States of America

It all started a long time ago when a friend took me to see my first **drag race.** As soon as the action on the **drag strip** started, I knew that I had found my sport. Even in those days there was plenty of action. It wasn't the super high-speed action like now. But it was good action, because just like now, all the guys did their best to run good races, build good cars, and turn good speeds. Maybe that's how come people say that drag racing is a sport for the good guys.

"Action" is the word for drag racing. It always has been and it always will be.

In those days there were lots of **stockers** and **super stock** models. The guys ran them down the drag strip between rows of hay bales. Plenty of hay bales got **wiped** when a driver got **squirrely** and **lost it.**

There were **spectators,** too. Mostly, the spectators were other drivers, friends, and people who just came and watched. Sometimes girl friends showed up.

The spectators stood behind the hay bales or a small fence. If a car got squirrely, the spectators scattered like a bunch of scared birds.

After a few accidents everyone in drag racing got interested in safety. I guess one of the biggest safety ideas to come along was the **rollbar.** First the guys had them in the faster **dragsters.** Pretty soon they put them in the little dragsters, super stocks, and **roadsters.**

It didn't take long before they got rid of those hay bales and put up strong fences. It wasn't that the guys got tired of eating hay. It was just that a few pounds of hay didn't do much to stop a car that was going over 100 miles an hour. In drag racing, we try to learn something from every accident.

In the early days of drag racing, people stood behind small fences or hay bales. Today, drag strips have heavy guardrails.

Early dragsters had rollbars, but they were not as heavy and strong as the rollbars used today.

Every time there was a drag meet, some smart cookie came up with something new to make a car go faster. I remember how all the guys really stared when the first **injectors** showed up. We all stood around and asked the owner, "Hey, what's with those pipes on your **carb**?"

When he told us how those pipes made more air go into the carb, mixed up more fuel, and made his car go faster, no one believed him.

After he took a few runs, everyone believed him.

Everyone ran to the shop to get a set of injectors. And every shop made injectors a different size and shape.

Injectors force more air and fuel into the carburetors. More air and fuel means more power.

At first, if a guy wanted to be in drag racing, he had to be his car's owner, driver, and mechanic, all in one. When it got so that it cost more to keep a car running in some of the faster **classes,** two or three guys would get together, build up a car, and make a team.

The guys on some teams took turns driving. On other teams, each person had a job like mechanic or driver. That's how I started. I did all the work. My friend did all the driving. For awhile I liked it that way. Then pretty soon I wanted to drive, too.

When the cars got faster and faster, we began to have more classes to keep the racing fair. Some of the classes were set by car speed. Other classes were set by the kind of engine or style of the car. When I first saw the rule book, it had more classes in it than a high school. But it's funny. The same guys who wouldn't read a school book sat down and read that rule book. I wonder how come.

The rule book told about safety, too. Some of the guys didn't like all the rules. But then, I don't know anybody who likes all the rules about anything, anyway.

A drag race team may be made up of the car's owner, the driver, mechanics, and friends.

In drag racing there are classes for almost every kind of car. This car could be in a class all its own.

At first in drag racing the cars ran in the 90's for speed and around fifteen seconds for **elapsed times, E. T.'s.** Pretty soon a few guys were cracking the hundred mile an hour mark. The E.T.'s started coming down, too, because of better tires and engines that could deliver quick power.

Once in awhile someone would talk about cracking the 200 mile an hour mark with an elapsed time under seven seconds. We all sat and stared at him like he'd flipped out.

"No one will ever do 200 miles an hour on the drag strip," we all said. Well, that's what we *said*.

The old dragsters were something to see. They were short, heavy, and had **flathead** engines. We used the flathead engine because that's the best there was.

An old dragster had a stiff **chassis.** Real solid. Some people called an old dragster a **rail.** A few people still call dragsters rails, but the chassis on a dragster today isn't stiff and solid, anymore. It isn't heavy, either. But drivers back in those days started **turning some pretty good times**—flathead engine, stiff chassis, and all.

Many drag-race models are very old cars—with very new engines. Some are models of forty-year-old cars.

An old dragster, sometimes called a rail, had a stiff chassis and a flathead engine. People call the flathead the granddaddy of drag racing engines.

For a long time the only use people had for **parachutes** was when they were coming *down* from someplace. After a few drivers got into trouble because their brakes failed at the end of a high speed run, a very smart cookie had a great idea. Why not use a parachute to help stop a car?

After awhile, drivers found out that for stopping a car at very high speed, a parachute worked better than brakes. That's because a **chute** gives a strong, steady pull on the back of a car. Brakes can fail or lock up and put a guy into a spin. A chute can fail too, so some drivers use two chutes, just in case!

Drag racing rules say that any car that goes over 150 miles per hour must *have a parachute for stopping it.*

Another thing I've always liked about drag racing is the way some of the cars look. In some classes, the cars are like nothing else. The cars in the **altered** class make people sit up and look twice.

The altered class got its name when people took a car and changed it, altered it. The altering got wilder and wilder until some models turned up with Ford bodies, Chevy engines, and handmade chassis. The altered cars were good to look at, but they also turned great speeds.

What makes drag racing really great is the people in it. Everyone helps everyone else. Like if a guy has a broken car, other people help him fix it or lend him parts. It's not like some stories that get around about someone trying to hurt another guy's car so he'll lose the race. Something like that may have happened somewhere, but it wasn't on the drag strip.

There have been some guys in drag racing who only wanted to win, no matter what. They only stayed a little while because there's more to drag racing than just winning.

An altered car looks like a model of some kind of car. Roadsters are very popular in the altered classes.

A drag race car is like any other racing car. Lots of work by the racing team to keep it going.

One important thing in drag racing is getting to the finish line and getting there in a hurry. If it's during **qualifying,** a driver wants to get to the finish line with a good enough E.T., or elapsed time, to put him into the **eliminations.**

If it's during eliminations, a driver wants to be at the finish line ahead of the other car. Going fast is important, but it's not enough.

The driver with the highest speed isn't the winner; the winner is the one who crosses the finish line first. That's what's most important. Well, maybe it's not *the* most important thing.

The winner of an elimination race goes on to race again. The loser is usually out of racing for the rest of the day.

For me, the most important thing is how a dragster is built. It should have a strong but springy chassis. That helps keep the front wheels on the ground where they belong. A driver doesn't get much steering control out of wheels that bounce up and down.

The dragster better have a **safety harness** and a good strong rollbar. At 200 miles an hour, it does a guy good to think that his rollbar will protect him in case he flips.

I guess dragster drivers are like everyone else. They say, "Nothing can happen to me." That's what they say, because that's what they hope.

In drag racing, there's something for everybody. By something, I mean some kind of a car. Now, I'm for dragsters. Other people like stockers or altereds. And then there are those wild **funny cars.**

I remember when they first started to show up. It wasn't long before a lot of dragster drivers changed to funny cars. But just the same, a lot of guys have stayed with the dragsters. Anyway there are meets for dragsters, meets for funny cars, and sometimes meets for everybody.

And with all the new people coming in, drag racing just keeps on growing and changing.

Every drag race car must have a harness for the driver. Some people say all cars should have harnesses.

The first funny cars were more for show than go, and some did long and high wheelies.

The first funny cars were great to look at but they weren't so great on speed. By using some of the ideas that we had learned in dragsters, funny car teams began coming up with cars that could really **haul.**

It took a long time before any dragster could get over that magic 200 mile an hour mark. After being around for only a few years, the funny cars are doing 200. Now the dragsters are trying for a new magic number—250 miles per hour. That's hauling!

I'll say drag racing keeps growing and changing! A few years ago most people didn't even know what a **VW** was. When someone brought a VW to the track, all the guys laughed. They don't laugh anymore. Now there are drag meets just for VW's. People call them Bug-Ins.

People don't laugh because when drivers get over 150 miles per hour out of a little four cylinder engine, that's big news. But that's the way it is on the drag strip. There's always something new and different coming along.

Today's funny cars are for both show and go. Two hundred miles per hour should be enough go for anyone.

Bug on the drag strip! Well, that's what drag racing is all about, a class for almost every kind of car.

One strange meet I'll never forget was the **diesel truck drags.**

Now I can't say that we saw any fantastic speeds or E.T.'s, but we saw some fantastic gear shifting, like ten times in a quarter mile. There was even a prize for the quickest gear shifter.

The drivers brought their big **rigs** to the track, lined up at the starting line, and smoked their way down the strip. Only they smoked their **stacks,** not their **slicks** the way we do on dragsters.

After I saw those diesel truck drags, knew there was something for everybody in drag racing.

Once a year there's a drag race meet for diesel trucks. There's a prize for the fastest and smoothest gear shifter.

For **bikers** we have motorcycle drag racing. People ride everything from little street or dirt bikes to giant twin engine **fuelers.**

The whole story of drag racing has happened again with **cycles.** At first people raced stock or street machines. Then they began adding **goodies** and making changes to get quicker and faster cycles. That meant more classes.

And there it is! A whole new sport, motorcycle drag racing. Now there are even drag racing meets and rules for the bikers. One motorcycle rule requires all riders to wear **leathers,** heavy pants and jackets, to protect riders.

Many people build special bikes just for drag racing. Drag cycles are some of the fastest in the world.

There are a lot of bikers in drag racing, but I'll tell you there aren't many **jet dragster** drivers. It had to happen, we all knew it would. So a few years ago, here comes someone with a **jet engine** dragster. Now there are probably not even a dozen jet dragster drivers in the country. But the jet drivers are the ones who can say they have gone from zero to 260 miles an hour in a little over six seconds. Those jets are something to see, especially at night.

The driver brings his jet car up to the starting line just like everyone else in drag racing. At first he just has the main jet engine going. When he's ready he cuts in the **afterburner.** That afterburner gives the extra power the dragster needs to **accelerate.**

It's easy to see why people call the jet dragsters **blowtorches.** At night one looks like a blowtorch on wheels.

The driver only needs the engine for a part of the quarter mile. But even that short jet burn will push the dragster over 260 miles per hour.

Jets hold all the drag racing records for speed and elapsed time. The jet engines are the same as those in jet aircraft.

Jet dragsters are called **blowtorches**. Does anyone want to roast a hot dog in the jet blast?

In the early days of drag racing, guys came out on the strip and drove in old clothes. We can still drive in any old clothes, but only in certain classes.

Just like the motorcycle rule on leathers, we have a rule about what we wear in classes where cars go over 150 miles per hour or use a special fuel. That rule says we have to wear a **firesuit,** helmet, gloves, and goggles. The car must have a safety harness, too.

A starting line official checks our goggles and safety harness before we make a run.

Drag racing rules say drivers of very fast cars with special fuels **must** *wear firesuits, face masks, and gloves.*

For a long time we could tell what kind of a run a car was making by the smoke from the slicks. Some drivers smoked off the starting line. Others kept the **hides** smoking halfway down the track. And the fantastic drivers smoked the hides all the way through the finish line **traps.** It takes a great car and driver to keep up the acceleration all the way through the quarter-mile run.

Then we got new tires with better **bite.** They were better for acceleration but they didn't smoke. Lots of us really miss those old days of smoking slicks.

Well, at least we can smoke the slicks when we do a **burn through.** To do our burn through, we have someone from the team put bleach or rosin on the track right in front of the slicks. Then we accelerate through the bleach. The spinning cleans the tires and warms them. It also leaves a little rubber on the track to give better bite.

With the kind of bite we get after doing a burn through, some dragsters and funny cars can turn speeds way over 200 miles an hour. Who said it would never happen?

When a driver has smoking slicks, people say he is **boiling the hides.** Some drivers used to boil the hides for a full quarter mile. Today's slicks don't smoke, because of a new kind of rubber used in the tires.

Drivers do burn throughs to clean and heat the slick tires before the quarter-mile run. Clean tires give better bite.

There are some of us in drag racing who like to stick with certain kinds of cars. Other guys drive anything that's new. My friends and I, we're dragster people. We're **injected** dragster people.

The funny cars are all right and the **blown** dragsters are all right, too. Funny cars and fuelers can turn speeds way over 200 miles per hour with six second E.T.'s.

Just the same, we stay with our little injected car. It's like an old friend. And besides, our kind of car can hit 200 miles per hour, too.

On a fast run it's the driver alone with his dragster and the drag strip.

For a long time, even years, things can go along great on the drag strip, and then one day, when a guy pushes for that 200 mark, it happens. Something goes squirrely and then the car is upside down, wiping out the timing lights and in big trouble. Even when it's happening a guy can't believe it.

There are some strange noises, too. Noises like metal screaming on the strip, glass crunching, a helmet pounding on the rollbar, and even with all the noise a kind of silence. The kind of silence where a man thinks, Is this really true? Is this how it is to be on the drag strip upside down?

When a car's in big trouble, there are some mighty wild things to see and feel. Flying glass, metal, parts, water, and oil make crazy scenery. But a guy doesn't get to see that scenery for very long. It all disappears in a cloud of dust or in a cloud of not knowing.

Before the scene is over, there are some feelings a driver won't forget if he lives to remember. Shaking, ripping, and tearing around the shoulder harness. Then the shaking gets far away, like a time when a guy's mom is waking him up to go to school.

Big trouble on the drag strip! The rest of the world watches and waits.

How long does an accident last? Only as long as it takes an accident to happen.

When there's big trouble on the strip, people move mighty fast. I guess the fastest guys around an accident are the other people on the dragster team. They may not believe what they see, but they still do all the right things in a hurry.

Even if all the help comes fast, it may seem like a long time to the driver, if he knows where he is. The dust clouds in the air and the dust clouds in his head might keep him from thinking anything. But if he knows where he is and what's going on, he'll think about one thing first.

If a guy in trouble has any time left or anything left to think with, he'll probably think, This isn't true, but if it is, I don't want to be here when all the fuel starts to burn.

Other people worry about the same thing, too. They're the guys that go for the fire extinguisher the minute anything goes wrong.

There are even some good guys at the drag strip who seem to know when something is about to go wrong. They have fire extinguishers in their hands before the trouble starts.

The first people to help after a driver has big trouble are the dragster's crew members.

Drag racing people grab fire extinguishers whenever there's big trouble on the drag strip.

After everyone has done what he can for the driver, he stands around, not sure what to do next. People wonder, What went wrong? What made the car flip? Was it all real?

They can't believe that in a few seconds a beautiful dragster has turned into a pile of junk. Everyone has a kind of blank feeling, like no feeling at all.

And everyone thinks about the driver. How does he feel? He feels bad for breaking up the dragster, but he feels glad to be there able to look at it.

I know, because it happened to me and I lived to tell about it. That's me, standing there in the firesuit. And I know I feel mighty thankful, too. Thankful for that rollbar.

"I'm awful sorry, guys, but I think I broke our beautiful dragster."

The good guys get to work, clean up, and haul away what's left of a beautiful machine. Now while they may not exactly like the clean up job, I can tell you I know exactly what they are thinking and what's going to happen.

Here's exactly how it will be. A few weeks after the trouble, the crew and driver will have a new car ready to run.

Now, some people leave drag racing and go into a different sport. Some don't stay in drag racing very long. But the rest of us, we stay. We race. We win some days, we lose on other days. Sometimes we have big trouble, but then we come back, because that's how it is on the drag strip. And that's the way we like it.

"But we'll be back on the drag strip, while the rest of the world watches and waits."

Glossary/Index

(Page number indicates where
the word first appears in the book)

Accelerate, p. 28   To gain speed.

Afterburner, p. 28   A second small jet engine inside the main jet engine used for extra acceleration.

Altered, p. 16   A car that has been changed so much that it looks only a little like the original model.

Bikers, p. 26   People who ride motorcycles.

Bite, p. 32   Traction or grip of tires on the drag strip.

Blown, p. 34   Supercharged. A supercharged engine has a pump to force extra air and fuel into the cylinder.

Blowtorch, p. 28   A small torch that shoots out a hot flame, made stronger by a blast of air.

Boiling the hides, p. 33   Making tires smoke.

Burn through, p. 32   A way of cleaning the tires on a drag race car. The driver spins the rear wheels of his car through a puddle of bleach or rosin.

Carb, Carburetor, p. 8   The part of an engine where air and fuel are mixed before going into the cylinders.

Chassis, p. 12   The main part of a car—the frame. All other parts are mounted on the chassis.

Chute, p. 14   Short for parachute.

Classes, p. 10   Groups of cars that run at about the same speed with similar engines and body styles.

Cycles, p. 26   Short for motorcyles.

Diesel truck drags, p. 24	A quarter mile race between large trucks.
Drag race, p. 4	A quarter mile race.
Dragster, p. 6	A car built for drag racing only.
Drag strip, p. 4	A straight flat quarter mile track.
Eliminations, p. 18	A race between two cars. Only the winner goes on to the next race. The car that wins the last race is the final elimination winner.
E.T., elapsed time, p. 12	The time it takes a car to cover the quarter mile.
Firesuit, p. 30	A suit made of cloth that does not burn easily.
Flathead, p. 12	An old style engine once very popular in drag racing. The top of the engine, which is called a head, is flat.
Fueler, p. 26	A motorcycle or car that uses fuel *other* than gasoline.
Funny car, p. 20	A car that looks like a new model but has been built only for drag racing.
Goodies, p. 26	Extra parts that make a car run better.
Haul, p. 22	Go fast.
Hides, p. 32	Drag racing talk for **tires.**
Injected, p. 34	A car with long tubes on the carburetor. *See* **Injectors.**
Injectors, p. 8	Long tubes on carburetors shaped in a way to force more air into the carbs. *See* **Carburetor.**
Jet dragster, p. 28	A dragster that uses an aircraft jet engine for power.
Jet engine, p. 28	The engine used on jet aircraft.
Leathers, p. 26	In motorcycle racing, a suit of heavy plastic or leather.
Lose it, lost it, p. 6	Lose control of a car.
Parachute, p. 14	A large, umbrella-shaped cloth used to stop a dragster and other drag racing cars.

Qualify, qualifying, p. 18	Making a timed run to place a driver in a class or a position in a class.
Rail, p. 12	Another name for a dragster.
Rig, p. 24	A large truck.
Roadster, p. 6	A very old, two-passenger car. A body style very popular in drag racing.
Rollbar, p. 6	A heavy steel bar shaped like a cage around the driver's seat to provide protection in case of accident.
Safety harness, p. 20	Strong straps that hold a driver in place.
Slicks, p. 24	Wide smooth tires that have no tread.
Spectators, p. 6	People who watch a race.
Squirrely, p. 6	A racing term meaning "out of control."
Stacks, p. 24	Tall exhaust pipes that reach above the cab of a diesel truck.
Stockers, p. 6	Regular cars that have not been greatly changed since they left the factory.
Super stock, p. 6	A regular car that has been made more powerful for drag racing.
Traps, p. 32	The timing lights at the end of the quarter mile dragstrip.
Turning a time, p. 12	The length of time it takes to make a run. The top speed at the end of a run.
VW, p. 22	Volkswagen—the small German car.
Wipe, wiped, p. 6	To lose a race or crash a car.

Ruth and Ed Radlauer, authors of over fifty books for young people, are graduates of UCLA. They have worked as teachers, school administrators, reading specialists, and instructors in creative writing. Their works include books in the areas of science, language, social studies and, more recently, high-interest reading materials. Along with their three children, two horses, a dog, and an ancient cat, the Radlauers live in La Habra, California.

The books in the Sports Action series are *On the Drag Strip, Scramble Cycle, Horsing Around, Buggy-go-Round, On the Sand, Chopper Cycle, Salt Cycle, Motorcycle Mutt, Bonneville Cars, On the Water, Foolish Filly,* and *Racing on the Wind.*

3